# NO MAN KNOWS MY PASTRIES

# NO MAN KNOWS MY PASTRIES

## THE SECRET *(NOT SACRED)* RECIPES OF

### SISTER ENID CHRISTENSEN

## AS TOLD TO

## ROGER S. SALAZAR & MICHAEL G. WIGHTMAN

Signature Books
Salt Lake City
1992

To Timmy Morrison,

for letting us take care of him
and helping us realize why we never want
children of our own.

LIBRARY OF CONGRESS CATALOGING-IN-PUBLICATION DATA

Salazar, Roger B.
    No man knows my pastries : the seceret (not sacred) recipes of
Sister Enid Christensen / Roger B. Salazar, Michael G. Wightman.
      p.   cm.
      ISBN 1-56085-028-0
      1. Cookery, Mormon. 2. Cookery—Utah. I. Wightman, Michael G.,
II. Title.
TX715.S1668   1992
   641.5'66—dc20                       92-16709
                                            CIP

# Contents

♥

*Our Eternal Family*

# *About the Author*

❤

A mong Mormons Sister Enid Christensen is a popular author, den mother, cook, and roll model. A prominent leader in the Payson, Utah, 227th Ward Relief Society, she has cooked countless inspirational meals and shared her testimony-strengthening culinary experiences with thousands of those weak in things of the kitchen.

There was the time, for example, when she was caught in a food-fight between Payson Troop 139 and Nagasaki Troop E=MC$^2$. Her chef's hat torn from her head by Jell-O and sushi projectiles, she escaped without so much as a wrinkle to her polyester dress.

Regarding this latter special experience, Sister Christensen remembers, "We were on all-night kitchen duty when the twenty-gallon pressure cooker exploded, sending showers of whole wheat shrapnel into my dear friend's kitchenette. Sister Brown caught a direct hit. I listened all night to her moans while fighting off two or three scouts who saw their chance for a midnight snack."

"When I found my companion, her head was barely above the wheat, which almost entirely filled the room. I counted sixty-seven wounds. 'If you ever have an opportunity . . . to talk to the young people of America,' she gasped, 'tell them it was an honor to cook for them. Tell 'em, "'Preciate cha.'"

Sister Christensen was born in Rexburg, Idaho; graduated from high school in 1966; attended hometown Ricks College that fall; transferred to the B.Y.U. the following semester; transferred to SUSC in the summer; transferred to Dixie College the next fall; and transferred to LDS Business College in the spring of 1968 where she met Brother LaMar Christensen. When their eyes met, they felt all tingly and knew that in the preexistence they had committed themselves to each other. They solemnized that promise three days later.

*A popular "roll" model*

Due to her righteous upbringing and Mormon values, Sister Christensen was soon hired by a four-star buffet restaurant, Le Cardinal, where she found not only fulfillment but the means to support a growing family. When Brother Christensen completed his education and launched a career as an accountant, Sister Christensen cheerfully abandoned hers. They eventually located in Payson, where Sister Christensen bore and raised five lovely children: LaRoy, LaRue, LaRee, LaRay, and Shirl.

Sister Christensen currently serves as Stake Relief Society Ancestral Recipe Coordinator.

*The gospel on KBYU and a Big Gulp—*
*it doesn't get better than this.*

# A Note from Brother Christensen
### (Enid's special half)

**T**o all sisters everywhere: You are good. You cook our meals, clean and make our homes. You hold us, doctor us, bless us, and try not to let us know how much smarter you are than we brethren. You do all of this within a tight budget. Necessity is the mother of invention, and throughout time you women have been ingenious and blessed by the Lord in making food stretch so that there will always be enough for everyone. I often wonder when Jesus fed the multitude if his dear, sweet mother Mary wasn't in the kitchen cooking.

Sisters, we are grateful and thankful that we have been blessed by your sweet spirits to serve us. We truly appreciate you.

IDAHO

❤ Shelley

❤ Malad

❤ Brigham City

West Valley City❤ ■ Park City

Wendover ■

❤ Lehi

❤ Nephi

❤ Moroni

❤ Manti

❤ Beaver

UTAH

❤ Hurricane

St. George❤

■ Colorado City

Las Vegas ■

❤ Joseph City

❤ Snowflake

ARIZONA

*The Jell-O Belt*

# Prelude

♥

**M**y dear brothers and sisters,

I would indeed be ungrateful if I didn't take this page to tell you how grateful and thankful I am to be able to bare my recipes. I feel so thankful to have been raised in the Jell-O Belt and not some foreign country where food doesn't matter. I hope and pray that these recipes, which I truly feel were inspired by the scriptures, church history, and family values, will inspire you too.

These recipes are tried and true. Trust the main recipes, for many of these are manna from heaven. If followed step by step, line upon line, ingredient upon ingredient, they will guide you to celestial success in your cooking. Just look at all the lovely recipes our own sweet Sister Janet Lee pioneered.

Have faith, persevere, be an example to the younger sisters in your ward. Become the culinary adventureress you were foreordained to be.

Your sister,
Enid Christensen

*A woman's work is never done.*

# My Body is a Temple . . .
# Not a Visitor's Center!

❤

**T**hroughout history we women have sought time-saving recipes. Now in the 1990s just about every way to prepare quick foods has been found. If you still use costly ingredients, then, sisters, welcome to the latter days! Cooking from scratch can add hours to otherwise quick dishes, leaving little time for church work and family. It can also add strange flavors and textures to foods, arousing taste buds in sensuous ways.

Cooking with prepared foods such as canned soups, boxed soups, crackers, and pastas saves time without sacrificing any man-made synthetic vitamins that help nourish and strengthen our bodies. Like satellites and fax machines, fast foods are a technological advance brought forth to assist in spreading the gospel.

Brothers and sisters, there are many reasons we have been blessed today with prepared foods. Fortunately many of these fine food companies are owned in part by the church. When we buy from them, we contribute even more tithing dollars.

Fast foods offer staying power. These starchy foods help keep our bodies warm all winter long. The insulative qualities of non-dairy whipped topping keeps Jell-O salad cool and congealed for hours longer than real whipped cream, a real boon for long funerals on hot summer days!

Brothers and sisters, join with me in stepping out of the past and into the conveniences of the future. Prepare and preserve your family's holy tabernacles with food that will take them into the Millennium.

Admonitions of love,
Sister Christensen

# JELL-O FLAVORS

| | Lemon | Lime | Strawberry | Raspberry | Orange |
|---|---|---|---|---|---|
| **carrots & celery** | picnic with the inlaws | Relief Society brunch; teen grounding | summer wedding buffet | Thanksgiving; hospital siege | any buffet or angelic visitation |
| **cottage cheese** | funeral or missionary reunion | anytime, anywhere | Swiss Days; Valentine dance | Christmas Eve dinner | revelation or Halloween party (add black jelly beans) |
| **mini marsh-mallows** | grand-parents' birthday (add prunes) | Polynesian baby blessing | Fourth of July picnic | Pioneer Day picnic | temple dedication; mall opening |
| **pineapple; coconut; banana** | senior citizen luau | Tongan ward dedication | ward banquet; missionary farewell | Christmas brunch; Marion stand-off | Samoan ward dedication |
| **fruit cocktail** | dinner on Monday | dinner on Tuesday | dinner on Wednesday | dinner on Thursday | dinner on Friday |

*ADDED INGREDIENTS* (vertical label at left)

*The Jell-O Matrix*

# Conversion Chart

| If the recipe calls for: | You may substitute: |
| --- | --- |
| whipped cream | non-dairy whipped topping |
| butter | margarine |
| coffee | Postum or Pero |
| white sauce | cream of mushroom soup |
| pasta or pastry crust | Ritz crackers |
| meat | Spam |
| steak sauce | ketchup or tomato soup |
| barbecue sauce | ketchup or tomato soup |
| red sauce | ketchup or tomato soup |
| tomato sauce | ketchup or tomato soup |
| spaghetti sauce | ketchup or tomato soup |
| wine | grape juice |
| liquor | ice cream |

*Well, there it is.*
*Jell-O's a hit every time.*

# There's Always Room for Jell-O Salad

❤

I dreamed a dream, and that's how the Jell-O Matrix was revealed to me! I am so pleased to share it with you in this very special Jell-O section. Jell-O is nature's wonder food. It not only strengthens your fingernails, it expands in your tummy to make you feel full.

The Jell-O matrix should be used to determine the proper Jell-O to serve for whatever occasion. Should you have a Jell-O salad already made, the matrix can be used in reverse to discover what party is awaiting you in your refrigerator.

Remember, Jell-O is that gay little lilt that turns any meal into a ward banquet. Good luck and happy jiggles.

# BANANA NUT JELL-O SALAD

1 pkg. strawberry Jell-O
1 can crushed pineapple
1 banana

2 tbsp. mayonnaise
2 tbsp. chopped, salted peanuts

As LaMar likes to remind me, it's the little things that make a big difference—like peanuts in Jell-O. Dissolve a small package of Jell-O in boiling water. Think about something inspirational like our Heavenly Father's drowning Pharaoh's charioteers in the Red Sea. Then add 1 cup cold water and chill. Don't get overanxious. Let it get gummy. Then measure 1 cup gelatin into a separate bowl and add the sliced banana. Spoon into individual molds and chill until set but not firm. Meanwhile blend mayonnaise into remaining gelatin. Add peanuts from your short-term food storage. Be sure they're salted. Spoon into molds. Chill until firm. Unmold. Makes 6 servings.

# JELL-O RIBBON LOAF

*A colorful and exciting snack for firesides!*

1 pkg. lime Jell-O
1 pkg. raspberry Jell-O
1 1/2 cups applesauce
18 double graham crackers

1 envelope Dream Whip
1/4 tsp. imitation almond extract
3 tbsp. confectioners' sugar
1/4 cup blanched almonds, toasted

A kaleidoscope of color in distinct layers! It's as fun as a lava lamp. Combine each small package of Jell-O with 3/4 cup applesauce each; stir each until well blended, about 1 1/2 minutes. Place 2 double crackers end to end on platter. Spread with 1/4 cup lime mixture. By now your mouth should be watering. Top with 2 double crackers and spread with raspberry mixture. Continue layers, alternating flavors and ending with crackers.

Prepare whipped topping mix as directed on package, using 1/4 teaspoon imitation almond extract instead of vanilla. Add confectioners' sugar. Spread over loaf. Sprinkle with almonds. Chill at least 30 minutes. Makes 12 to 14 servings. Better make 2 loaves because they go fast.

# JELL-O BIRTHDAY SURPRISE

1 large pkg. or 2 small pkgs. of your
   favorite Jell-O
1 pint vanilla ice cream

1 pint strawberry ice cream
marshmallows and gumdrops

Surprise! Jell-O for your birthday! What an unexpected treat. Dissolve Jell-O in 2 cups boiling water. Add 1 1/2 cups cold water. Pour into a 1-quart ring mold and chill until firm. Unmold (run the inverted mold under hot water) and fill center of ring with lots of ice cream. Place marshmallows and gumdrops around gelatin, using gumdrops as holders for birthday candles.

Makes 6 servings, depending on the birthday boy or girl. When it's my birthday, I make three. We sing this little tune before blowing out the candles (be sure to sing quickly before the Jell-O melts):

> Jell-O, Jell-O birthday, children dear!
> Jiggly days will come to you all year.
> If I had one wish then it would be,
> A Jell-O, Jell-O birthday to you from me.

# FROZEN JELL-O AMBROSIA

1 pkg. orange Jell-O
1/4 tsp. salt
2 tbsp. sugar
2 oranges, peeled and sectioned

1 cup Dream Whip
1 1/3 cups flaked coconut
1 tsp. grated orange rind
2 tbsp. Miracle Whip

If the ancient Greeks had non-alcoholic Jell-O ambrosia, they wouldn't have gotten into so much mischief. Still, don't overdo it with this beguiling temptress. To begin take a small package of Jell-O and dissolve in boiling water along with the salt and sugar. Drain orange sections, measuring juice and adding cold water to make 1 cup. Add to gelatin. Chill until thick. Fold in the Dream Whip, coconut, oranges (peeled and sectioned), orange rind, and Miracle Whip (Now *there's* something the Greeks didn't have). Pour into tray and freeze until firm. Makes 6-8 servings. Cool!

*We hope and pray you will love it, too.*

# JELL-O FRUIT DESSERT ELEGANT

*Telestially delicious!*

1 small pkg. raspberry Jell-O
1 tbsp. sugar
1/8 tsp. salt
1 10 oz. pkg. frozen raspberries,
    thawed

1 can crushed pineapple
1 cup sour cream
2 medium bananas
1 cup miniature marshmallows
1 cup chopped walnuts

I put my family in the right mood for this special dish by using a French accent on *"daay-zer el-aye-gahnt."* In addition to Jell-O, dissolve sugar and salt in 1 cup boiling water. Drain raspberries and pineapple, reserving 3/4 cup of the combined syrups. Resist the temptation to drink this before you add it to the gelatin. Chill until thick, whip until fluffy, and beat sour cream until smooth. When everything has reached its predestined state, fold in gelatin mixture. Then stir in fruits, marshmallows, and walnuts. Chill about 15 minutes. Stir and spoon into a 2-quart mold or bowl and chill until firm. Unmold and spoon into dessert dishes before serving. Makes 8-10 healthy and attractive servings. Bon appetite!

# FIG AND ORANGE JELL-O MOLD

1 pkg. lemon Jell-O
1/4 tsp. salt
1 tbsp. lemon juice

1/2 cup dried figs
1 cup diced orange sections

The parable of the withered tax collector and the withered fig tree comes to mind. That's why I serve this at tax time. It cheers LaMar up to know what our Heavenly Father truly thinks of the IRS.

Dissolve Jell-O and salt in 1 cup boiling water. Add 3/4 cup cold water and lemon juice and chill until thick. Meanwhile cover figs with boiling water, let stand 10 minutes, drain, remove stems, cut into fine strips, and fold figs and oranges into gelatin. Pour into 1-quart mold. Chill until firm. Unmold. Best served with whipped topping. Makes 6 servings.

*All this and heaven, too.*

# CELESTIAL JELL-O CHEESE MOLD

| | |
|---|---|
| 1 small pkg. lcmon or lime Jell-O | 2 1/2 tsp. seasoned salt |
| 1/2 cup sour cream | 3/4 tsp. Worcestershire sauce |
| 2 1/2 cups cottage cheese | 1/2 tsp. lemon juice |
| 4 oz. bleu cheese | 2 tbsp. minced chives |

This is my favorite Jell-O recipe of all, and I try to save it for extra-special occasions such as bridal showers and Eagle Scout Courts of Honor. Try matching the Jell-O color to the crêpe paper decorations.

Begin by dissolving the Jell-O in 3/4 cup boiling water. Chill until very thick. Meanwhile, combine remaining ingredients except the chives and beat until smooth. Add the gelatin, blending well. Fold in the chives. Pour into a 1-quart mold and chill until firm. Unmold. Serve as an appetizer with assorted crackers and fresh vegetables. Don't prepare Celestial Cheese Mold if you're on a diet, because you won't be able to just nibble.

# LIME JELL-O SALAD

| | |
|---|---|
| 1 pkg. lime Jell-O | dash of pepper |
| 1 tsp. salt | dash of paprika |
| 1 cup cottage cheese | 1 tbsp. finely chopped onion |
| 1 cup buttermilk | 1/2 cup finely chopped celery |
| 1 tsp. white vinegar | 1/4 cup thinly sliced radish |
| 1 tbsp. horseradish | |

Not every Jell-O salad has to be tutti-frutti, and lime Jell-O is particularly suited to vegetables, cheeses, and candies. What a surprise when people bite into this jiggly garden treat at ward parties. Don't worry. Those with cultured palettes will bear you off on their shoulders.

To work this miracle, dissolve a small package of Jell-O and salt in 3/4 cup boiling water. Cool to room temperature. Beat cheese until smooth, then stir the buttermilk, vinegar, horse-radish, pepper, paprika, and cheese into the gelatin. Chill until very thick, add remaining ingredients, and pour into a 1-quart mold. Chill until firm. Unmold. Makes 8 side salads. You may also add anchovies, bleu cheese, scallions, and kippers.

*When no one's home . . .*

# Miracle Whip of Forgiveness
# Salads and Salad Dressings

♥

**O**vereating! The original sin! We sisters have paid for Eve's eating disorder long enough. If you think you've overdone it, whip up one of my high-roughage salads and don't worry. My whole life I was too thin, and now thanks to my deep faith and the strength that Heavenly Father has given me, my anorexia is now in remission. Finally I have the rounder and softer celestial characteristics of the mature Mormon goddess.

# JOY PEACH SALAD

*Dressing:*
1/2 tsp. salt
dash pepper
2 tbsp. sugar
2 tbsp. vinegar
1/4 cup extra-virgin olive oil
dash tabasco
1 tbsp. snipped parsley

*Salad:*
1/4 cup sliced almonds
1 tbsp. sugar
1 cup chopped celery
2 green onions with tops,
  thinly sliced
1 cup diced peaches, drained
1 head romaine lettuce, torn into
  bite-sized pieces

This recipe is named in honor of my dear, civic-minded friend, Joy Peach, who almost single-handedly founded the My Family Lasts Forever, How About Yours? Foundation. For our unmarried brothers and sisters, take two white candles, Robert Goulet's latest album, Joy Peach Salad, and a bottle of your favorite non-alcoholic Cold Duck, then pop the question. It worked for me!

Mix the dressing ingredients and shake together vigorously in a zipper-lock bag. We're not talking a romp-with-a-salad-tumbler. Really shake this up. After your workout, refrigerate and add to the salad just before serving.

Cook your almonds in sugar over low heat, stirring constantly until sugar is dissolved and almonds are coated. Cool the almonds and break apart. Store at room temperature. The lettuce, green onions, and celery can be refrigerated together in a plastic bag. To serve, combine all ingredients.

# UNCLE BRUCE'S FRUIT DRESSING

1 small can frozen orange juice       1 tsp. vanilla

1 cup sour cream                      1 tsp. nutmeg

8 oz. cream cheese

I find that our sisters often want to know the appropriate attire for foods. In this case, something loose-fitting and comfortable with stylish, sensible shoes.

Mix all the ingredients in a food processor until smooth. It goes with any salad. And remember, pearls before five, never!


# TABOO-LI

1 cup bulgur wheat (fine)             1/2 cup lemon juice

1 cucumber, diced                     1/4 cup oil

2 tomatoes, diced                     1 1/2 tsp. salt

2 medium onions, diced                1/2 tsp. pepper

15-20 parsley sprigs, minced          2 tbsp. mint, pulverized

This is a glorious dish LaMar and I picked up on our Holy Land tour. Wash bulgur wheat 2-3 times. While the bulgur's soaking, treat yourself to an hour-long, much-deserved bath. Try it. If you are tempted by stray thoughts, just sing a hymn. After an hour, drain and mix the vegetables with the wheat. Then add the dressing and spices. Mix. How special this dish can be if you refrain from indulging until the spices are the most potent!

*Brethren, don't think for one moment*
*we sisters aren't aware of what you're up to.*

# ARTIE'S CHOKE CHICKEN SALAD

2 cups cooked, diced chicken

1 can artichokes, diced

1 cup peeled, diced celery

1 cup chunk pineapple

1 cup seedless green grapes

3/4 cup mayonnaise

2 tbsp. lemon juice

Art, from Blackfoot, Idaho, shared this recipe with LaMar as a teenager. I've since taken the liberty of adding grapes to spice it up a little. LaMar always gets a kick out of it. Mix all ingredients together and serve on a bed of lettuce.


# FRUIT SALAD COCKTAIL

1 large can fruit cocktail, drained

1/2 pkg. mini marshmallows

1 large container non-dairy topping

1 cup nuts

I believe it's the staples that hold us together, and this is one of the most staple—you can never have too much on hand. When friends or family pop in, serve them a cocktail. Mix and chill. May be doubled or tripled for family gatherings.

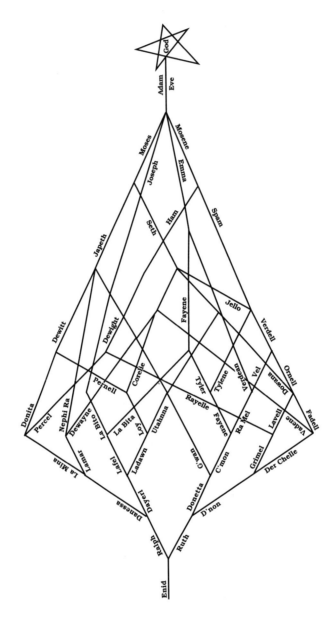

*Our Family Tree*

# In-Breads

**M**y commitment is to be always on the cutting edge of culinary fashion. My scouts work the wards and scour the stakes to find up-to-the-minute bread recipes. It is important to know which breads are in and which breads are out. We in the church are mainly concerned with the "in-breads."

Bread, a staple, the very staff of life, the beginning of the food chain, reminds me of the tree of life. In our church, and especially in Utah, I am reminded of another basic tree—the genealogical tree. Many states have had to pull from a gene pool. But thanks to plural marriage we are a simpler people. We draw our fair skin and blond hair from the Utah gene puddle.

You may notice that LDS family trees come to a point or are conifer-shaped rather than the deciduous branching out of the gentile family tree. But know in your heart that this characteristic separates us from the gentile world and keeps us special.

Due to our special polygamous heritage—the tireless work of numerous sisters—we have inherited hundreds of bread, gluten, and whole wheat recipes that put the rest of the world to shame. Pound for pound, the Mormon staff tips the scale every time over the over-rated French imposture, sliced or unsliced. Of course I have improved on the basics, so here are some exotic variations on a theme.

*Give us this day our daily bread.*

# MOUNT OF OLIVES NUT BREAD

## (Matthew 24:3)

2 1/2 cups flour
4 tsp. baking powder
1 egg, beaten

1 cup sliced, stuffed green olives
1 cup chopped walnuts

The key to this dish is not to confuse Mount of Olives with a mound of olives, because you need some packaging to keep the goodies from falling out.

First, sift the flour, sugar, baking powder, and salt. Then combine the eggs and milk, add to the rest and mix until moist. Then suffer the olives and nuts to come into the mixture. Turn into 8 1/2-inch round pan, bake at 350 degrees for 45 minutes, remove from pan, and cool. Serve with butter, or better yet cream cheese, which has only half the calories so you can use twice as much. (Butter and cream cheese together can be fabulous.)


# I KNEAD THEE EVERY HOUR KOLACHES

1 cup luke warm milk
1/2 cup sugar
1 tsp. salt
2 eggs

2 yeast cakes dissolved in 1/4 cup
 water
1/2 cup shortening, melted
4 1/2 to 5 cups flour
1/2 tsp. mace (not the aerosol)

When you hear kolaches, think galoshes, because wet and sticky is the secret to these sweet rolls. Mix the milk, sugar, salt, and eggs, then mix the remaining ingredients and crumble them in. Knead and let rise, then punch down. Let rise again, and punch down. Grease cookie sheets, make 2-inch balls, and let rise on cookie sheets. When light, make depression and fill with prunes, peaches, cherries, poppy seeds, or any combination. Bake at 350 degrees for about 20 minutes.

*My kulch-ral refinement lesson.*

# SIN-O-MEN ROLLS

## *Exceedingly Nummy!*

| | |
|---|---|
| 3/4 cup scalded milk | 1 tsp. salt |
| 3/8 cup shortening | 2 pkg. yeast added to 1 cup warm |
| 3 eggs, beaten | water |
| 6-7 cups flour | butter |
| 3/4 cup sugar | cinnamon |

Sunday afternoon in the park with Sin-O-Men Rolls is about as nummy as it gets. After church meetings, of course.

Preparation is straightforward as long as you aren't tempted to stray from the recipe. Mix sugar, shortening and salt slowly into scalded milk and let cool slightly. Mix eggs with milk mixture. Add yeast mixture, stirring well. Add 6 cups flour, knead well. Add final flour to adjust texture. Let rise. Punch down, let rise again. Roll out on floured surface. Butter lightly and sprinkle cinnamon on dough. Roll up, cut, place in a jelly roll pan and bake at 350 degrees until lightly browned on top. A glass of cold milk, and who could resist?

# A MARVELOUS WORK WITH WONDER BREAD

| | |
|---|---|
| 1 egg | 1 unsliced loaf, cut into 3" cubes, |
| 1/4 lb. softened butter | frozen |
| | 1 glass sharp cheddar cheese spread |

Let's face it, white bread can be pretty boring, like living in Vernal, Utah. To spice it up, try this. Mix egg, butter, and cheese. Smother the bread cubes with the egg, butter, and cheese mix. Frost all sides except bottom. Bake at 325 degrees until golden brown. Serve with chicken or tuna fish salad.

*Noth'n says lov'n like something from the ov'n,*
*and my hot buns say it best!*

# BUBBLE BUNS

1 24 oz. pkg. frozen yeast rising
   dough (2 doz. per pkg.)
1 3 oz. pkg. butterscotch pudding
   mix

1/2 cup chopped pecans
1/2 cup melted butter
1/2 cup brown sugar

The inspiration for these comes from Brother Freiberg's famous paintings. Start with a greased bundt pan. Cut the frozen rolls into halves. (Be careful. Stick point of knife in and pry each bun in half.) Put buns on bundt pan and sprinkle with pecans. Mix the dry pudding and brown sugar, and sprinkle over the buns. Then drizzle melted butter over all. Cover with plastic wrap. Let rise overnight or eight hours and bake at 325 degrees for 25 minutes. When baked, invert on plate. These adorable sticky buns will be devoured on sight.

# JAREDITE BANANA BOAT BREAD

1 cup flour
1 tsp. soda
1 cup whole wheat flour
3/4 cup brown sugar
3 medium bananas

1/4 cup plain yogurt
1 tsp. baking powder
1/4 tsp. salt
1 stick butter
1 egg

We know from the Book of Mormon that before Nephites and Lamanites there were Jaredites who traveled to Mexico. We may not know exactly what Jared's boats looked like, but I had a vision of their artistic potential in bread while crafting plastic grapes at Relief Society.

To begin this voyage, sift white flour, baking powder, baking soda, and salt on wax paper. Add whole wheat flour and mix. Cream butter and brown sugar well. Add egg, mix well. Combine mashed bananas and yogurt and add to butter mixture. Stir this into flour mixture only until blended. Then fashion your boat. Bake at 350 degrees for 50-55 minutes in a 9x5x3 pan. Don't peek while the buoys are baking or you'll be left with dinghies.

*You won't find these sitting on the plains.*

# MOUNTAIN MEADOWS MUFFINS

| | |
|---|---|
| 1 15 oz. pkg. raisin bran | 1 qt. buttermilk |
| 1 cup salad oil | 5 tsp. soda |
| 3 cups sugar | 2 tsp. salt |
| 4 eggs | 5 cups flour |

I am indebted to the Lee family of southern Utah for graciously sharing this recipe with me. Their neighbors, the Haights, have a different memory of the ingredients, but the Lee version is easier to swallow. Follow the instructions carefully and the brethren will massacre these.

To begin, mix raisin bran (my substitute for desert herbs), sugar, flour, soda, and salt in an extra large bowl. I use a special bowl commemorating the Utah War. Add oil, eggs, and buttermilk. Mix well. Store in covered containers in refrigerator. When you get around to it, bake the dough in greased muffin tins 2/3 full at 400 degrees for 15 to 20 minutes. Makes about 4 quarts of dough. Some of the brethren prefer a little ketchup on these.

# POPPYCOCK BREAD

| | |
|---|---|
| 1 Butter Brickle Cake Mix | 1 cup hot water |
| 1 box instant coconut pudding | 1/4 cup oil |
| 1/4 cup poppy seeds | 4 eggs |

A warning for you California Saints: Don't try gathering your own poppy seeds. LaMar and I discovered one vacation to Anaheim just how potent California poppy seeds can be. ("Poppies, poppies, to put them to sleep.") We do harvest our own mushrooms and snails, though. To prepare, simply mix all ingredients and cook in small, greased loaf pans and bake at 350 degrees until done.

# PINEAPPLE NUT BREAD

*Served in the Luau Room in the Hawaiian temple!*

| | |
|---|---|
| 3/4 cup brown sugar | 1/2 tsp. salt |
| 2 eggs | 1 can (8 1/2 oz.) crushed pineapple |
| 2 tsp. baking powder | 3/4 cup chopped nuts |
| 1/4 tsp. soda | 2 tbsp. sugar |
| 3 tsp. soft butter | 1/2 tsp. cinnamon |
| 2 cups flour | |

When the Lamanites traveled to Polynesia they took with them many plain and precious recipes. Through the years many things were added to and taken away from these recipes. After much prayer, fasting, and conversation with Thor Hyerdahl, I have restored this recipe to its original purity. Set the mood by playing a Don Ho album.

Cream brown sugar, butter, and eggs until fluffy. Blend dry ingredients and stir half into the creamed mixture. Add pineapple and juice, then the remaining dry mixture. Blend in nuts. "Lei" the mixture in a 9x5x3 loaf pan and sprinkle with sugar and cinnamon mixture. Bake 60-70 minutes at 350 degrees. Put on your grass skirt and serve. *Aku, aku!*

# Cheeses of Nazareth
# Appetizers and Dips

❤

**C**ultured dairy products came from the Middle East, not just from Cache Valley as some of our northern Utah Saints like to think. I just imagine the boy Jesus coming home from school to a toasted cheese sandwich, a glass of cold goat's milk, and yogurt dessert. Thank goodness for today's conveniences such as processed, pasteurized cheese products, which can add substance to almost any dish without lengthy preparation or aging.

*Search the papers diligently,
for in them you will find coupons.*

# YOUR FAVORITE PROCESSED CHEESE DIP

1 lb. Velveeta cheese

1 medium can evaporated milk

1 medium jar stuffed olives, cut in thirds

It doesn't need to be expensive to be celestial. A quiet evening at home in front of the T.V. with plenty Processed Cheese Dip to keep the kids at bay . . . .

To realize this heaven on earth, heat the cheese and milk over low heat until cheese is melted and mixture is bubbly and thick, stirring constantly. Add olives, let cool. This dip also doubles as a sauce for hot dogs or tortilla chips.

# CHEESE PUFFS

1 cup cheddar cheese, grated

1/4 cup butter

3/4 cup sifted flour

1/4 cup water

Fresh home-made Cheetos are just the thing for lackluster Family Home Evenings. Have the kids help mold the dough into life-like figures of their favorite Super Heros, teachers, and church leaders.

Mix the grated cheese with butter, cut in flour, and knead. Add water. Mold mixture into shapes and place on cookie sheet. Bake at 400 degrees for 15 minutes, then cool. You can also mold the dough around olives or use olives for heads.

# BEEFY JERKY

2 pkgs. dried beef  
1 8 oz. pkg. cream cheese  
1 lb. Velveeta cheese  

garlic salt  
celery salt  
onion salt  

Great-grandfather DeVerl used to pack this in his saddlebag when he'd ride out looking for wives. It sustained him through nine courtships. I have modernized the recipe for convenience.

Spread 2 packages of dried beef on a rectangular cookie sheet, covered with aluminum foil. Melt the cream cheese and Velveeta cheese and spread over the dried beef. Cool slightly and roll up. Wrap in foil and freeze, then cut into rounds. Garnish with garlic, onion, and celery salts. Then place in your fanny pack and see what develops. (You may substitute Turkey Jerky, if desired.)

# SUGARED BACON BITS

1 lb. bacon  

brown sugar  

The thing about this surprising snack is that it is so nutritious. You get red meat, brimming with protein, and polysaccharides for energy all in one simple dish.

Cut bacon slices in thirds and place in a jelly roll pan on foil, shiny side up. Sprinkle bacon generously with brown sugar and bake at 400 degrees for 15 minutes. Serve cooled.

# CHEESE ZEST SOUP

| | |
|---|---|
| **5 tbsp. melted butter** | **4 tbsp. flour** |
| **1/2 cup chopped celery** | **4 cups chicken broth** |
| **1/2 cup chopped onion** | **2 cups cheddar cheese** |
| **1/2 cup chopped carrot** | **1 cup Velveeta** |

For a little pick-me-up mid-day, try Velveeta cheese soup. Cook the butter, celery, onion, and carrots until tender, then add the flour and stir well. Next add the chicken broth, cook until thickened, add cheddar cheese, cook until melted, add Velveeta, and cook until melted.

This soup gets me through Richard Simmons and "All My Children." Avoid cold soda pop as a beverage, especially if you have a weak stomach, which can add too much zest and can also form a disagreeable ball of dairy fat in your stomach.

# CLAM DIGGERS DIP

| | |
|---|---|
| **8 oz. cream cheese** | **1/2 tsp. Worcestershire sauce** |
| **1 tbsp. mayonnaise** | **8-10 drops Tabasco sauce** |
| **1 tsp. instant onion** | **milk for desired consistency** |
| **1 tbsp. lemon juice** | **1 can drained clams** |
| **1/2 tsp. garlic salt** | |

Some sisters complain about having to dig for fresh clams. I've never understood why, since my clams have always behaved themselves. For the squeamish, use canned clams. Add all ingredients to a large pot and allow to simmer for an hour. Serve with chips and your favorite non-alcoholic malt beverage.

*Mormon Gothic*

# TEMPLE SQUARES

**1 6 oz. jar marinated artichoke hearts, drained and cut**
**1 lb. Monterey jack cheese, grated**

**4 beaten eggs**
**1 lb. cooked, drained, crumbled bacon**

Great canapés for Jewish weddings. We take them to Temple Square to enjoy while listening to General Conference, which is broadcast to picnickers outside.

Use an 8-inch pyrex pan sprayed with Pam. Spread artichokes in pan, spread cheese over top and sprinkle bacon on top of the cheese. Bake at 250 degrees for 45 minutes.

# MOON BALLS

**1 cup nonfat dry milk**
**1/2 cup honey**

**1/2 cup peanut butter**
**toasted wheat germ**

Yum! Who would have thought health food could be so tasty. People ask me how I come up with such imaginative combinations. Well, designing recipes isn't for amateurs or the faint-hearted.

Combine all the ingredients except the wheat germ. Form into balls, roll in wheat germ, and chill. Then eat your fill. The more you eat, the lighter you feel, which is why I call them moon balls.

*Tomorrow he gets oysters.*

# PEARL OF GREAT SPICE

**8 oz. pkg. cream cheese**
**1 cup sour cream**
**1 pkg. dry onion soup mix**

**1 can smoked oysters, drained on**
**paper towel and chopped**
**1 handful chopped nuts**

When your husband's get-up-and-go has got-up-and-gone, oysters are the remedy. Mix all the ingredients together and serve with crackers.

# SHRIMP DIP

**8 oz. cream cheese**
**1 can small shrimp**

**1 can cream of mushroom soup**

LaMar is sometimes sensitive about his size—even though I tell him he's big enough for me—and when he's feeling small I say, "LaMar, how about some shrimp dip?" That cheers him right up. Combine the cream cheese, shrimp, and soup and serve.

# BETHLE-HAM AND CHEESE SANDWICHES

6 pita bread rounds

2 cups chopped ham (you may
   substitute turkey ham)

1/2 cup Miracle Whip

1 cup crumbled feta cheese

shredded lettuce

A treat for Jew or gentile! Mix the ham, Miracle Whip, and feta together. Load the pitas and add the lettuce.


# HOT HAMBURGER DIP

3 lbs. hamburger, browned and
   drained

1 cup chopped green pepper

2 cups chopped onions

2 cups sliced green olives

1 bottle capers

2 cups raisins

3/4 cup red grape juice

1 tsp. garlic powder

1 tsp. Accent

1/2 tsp. oregano

1 tsp. salt

1/2 tsp. pepper

1/2 tsp. paprika

This isn't a dip for hamburgers. It's for nachos, hot dogs, and whatever else strikes your fancy. Mix everything together and simmer for 40 minutes. If you want it really hot, add jalapeños.

# 'Til We Meat Again

♥

As our precious Word of Wisdom says in the scriptures, eat meat sparingly unless there's a food shortage, then it's all right to eat more. In our family we eat meat once a day, but some will want to indulge more. Everyone needs whole proteins, otherwise our stomachs would distend like those poor, unfortunate people in *National Geographic.* These days people are tired of steak and potatoes and crave more sophisticated dishes like casseroles.

I find that presentation is nine-tenths of a casserole. My three rules are: Chips, Chips, Chips. Corn chips and Doritos for ethnic casseroles and old-fashioned chips for tuna and mushroom dishes. As I was baking recently, LaMar composed a little song in honor of my casserole talent. It's called, "Casserole-serole," to the tune of "Que Será Será":

When I was just a little boy
I asked my father, "What did we eat?
Did we eat pork chops?
Did we eat steak?"
Here's what he said to me:

"Casserole-serole!
Whatever was in it, we ate it.
Your mother's the one who made it,
Casserole-serole."

*"Casserole-serole . . . ."*

# FLAKY MORMON CASSEROLE

| | |
|---|---|
| 1 can green beans | 1 can french fried onion rings |
| 1 can cream of mushroom soup | 1 cup coarsely broken potato chips |

This is a sure-fire winner at ward dinners. If you bring this to any smorgasbord, you will be swamped with requests for the recipe.

Pour the green beans and soup into a 9x9 pan. Stir until evenly mixed, and sprinkle the potato chips and onion rings on top. Bake at 350 degrees for 20-25 minutes. Don't let stand too long or the chips will be leathery.


# SWEET AND SOUR SPAM

| | |
|---|---|
| 2 cans Spam, diced | 1/4 cup vinegar |
| 2 tbsp. fat | 1 cup pineapple juice |
| 1/4 cup water | 1 tbsp. soy sauce |
| 2 tbsp. cornstarch | 3/4 cup green pepper, cut in strips |
| 1/2 tsp. salt | 1/4 cup thinly sliced onion |
| 1/4 cup brown sugar | 1 can pineapple chunks |

Today's home-makers are indeed grateful to Hormel for the secrets that go into the incredible manufacture of Spam. How they can sell a ready-to-eat meat product for less than a raw ham is one of life's many blessings. I'll bet even Moses would have approved.

After you dislodge the meat from the can—a small price to pay for working with this special product, brown the Spam in hot fat, add water, cover, and simmer 1 hour. Combine cornstarch, salt, brown sugar, vinegar, pineapple juice and soy sauce. Mix and cook, stirring until slightly thick. Pour sauce over hot Spam and let stand at least 10 minutes. Add green pepper, onion, and pineapple chunks; cook a few minutes. Serve with rice.

*Have you ever been to Mammoth Cave?*

# YOU-CAN-STUFF-IT FRENCH BREAD LOAF

1 loaf french bread
1 lb. browned hamburger, drained
1 medium onion, chopped
1 green pepper, chopped

1 can cheese soup
1/2 cup canned milk
crumbled bread from hollowed out
  loaf

At Relief Society I taught a Cultural Refinement lesson on France and taught the sisters to say, *"Le pain, c'est bon."* When I served them French Bread Loaf fresh from the oven, you should have heard them shriek, *"C'est bon, c'est bon!"*

For your own cultural refinement, hollow out the French bread and set aside, saving the top. Combine the ingredients and simmer on low heat in a pan to heat through. Fill the bread, put top on, wrap in foil, and heat in oven 15 minutes at 350 degrees. *Que c'est bon!*

# TERIYAKI STEAK SANDWICHES

12 French baguettes
1 cup soy sauce
3/4 cup vegetable oil
3 tbsp. chopped onion

1 clove garlic, crushed
3 tbsp. brown sugar
6 lbs. beef skirt steaks

Teriyaki steak sandwiches may sound a bit carnal, sensual, and devilish, but they're really just wholesome all-American cows dressed up in exotic oriental costumes.

In a large, flat baking dish or plastic container, combine the soy sauce, vegetable oil, onion, garlic and brown sugar; stir to dissolve the sugar. Add steaks to the marinade, turning to coat well. You may be tempted to cook them right away, but they need to be refrigerated at least 2 hours to absorb the spices. Then grill the steaks over hot coals, 6-7 minutes on each side for medium-well done. Cut them into pieces and serve on the baguettes.

*Sheep Dogs keep a man at home.*

# SHEEP DOGS

**1 dozen hot dogs**                   **2 cups shredded cheese**
**6 cups mashed potatoes (instant)**

Wooly weenies are meant for the out-of-doors. For the deer hunt, Superbowl Sunday, or a pinewood derby, Sheep Dogs divert the brethren's attention from male bonding to lunch.

When you need to ride herd, get a dozen hot dogs and slice them lengthwise without cutting through. Place on a baking sheet. Spoon 1/2 cup mashed potatoes into each slit. Top with cheese and bake at 350 degrees for 20 minutes. When the dogs are sizzling and the cheese is melted, whistle your men to the table.

# BOLOGNA ANGEL WINGS

**1 lb. sliced bologna**                   **toothpicks**
**1 bottle green olives**

For a Christmas hors-d'oeuvre, cut the bologna slices as indicated in the diagram:

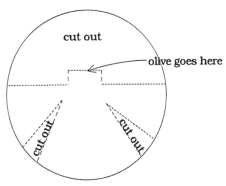

Place an olive on top, and bake at 350 degrees until crisp on the edges. Serve on a cloud of mashed potatoes.

*You ate what, where?*

# SAUSAGE SOUFFLÉ

| | |
|---|---|
| 1/4 lb. sausage | 1 pat butter |
| 1 cup cheddar cheese, grated | 1 egg |
| 1 slice bread | 1/4 cup milk |

This is my most elegant entree. Long-stemmed roses, candles, and Corelle dinnerware are in order for this lovely dish.

Place buttered bread side down in a casserole dish. Brown the sausage and sprinkle it and cheese over the bread. Top with another slice of bread, buttered side up. Mix egg and milk, pour over the sandwich, and squish down until absorbed. Generously sprinkle grated cheese on top. Cover with plastic wrap and put in refrigerator overnight. Bake at 350 degrees for 40 minutes. Makes one soufflé per person.

# FRANKED CORN THINGS

| | |
|---|---|
| 2 eggs | 3/4 cup milk |
| 1 cup grated parmesan cheese | 3/4 tsp. salt |
| 1 tsp. celery seed | 1/4 tsp. garlic salt |
| 5 hot dogs, sliced | 1/4 cup chopped onion |
| 1 14 oz. pkg. corn muffin mix | 1/4 cup cooked, crumbled bacon |

Hot dogs may be our most versatile meat product. If you substitute corn flakes for the muffin mix (as I know some of you will), you will need to increase the milk portion to 1 cup. Combine all ingredients and pour into a greased jelly roll pan. Bake at 400 degrees for 20 minutes or until golden brown.

# STUFFED HAMBURGER BIRDS

| | |
|---|---|
| 1 1/2 lbs. hamburger | 1/4 cup butter |
| 1 1/2 tsp. salt | 2 tbsp. lemon juice |
| 1 cup Hamburger Helper | 1/4 tsp. black pepper |
| 1 medium onion, grated | |

Your guests will think you have prepared stuffed chicken breasts. The secret is to flatten the hamburger, blended well with the salt in a medium bowl, into twelve paper-thin patties. Use waxed paper to smoosh them as thin as possible. In a small bowl, add the remaining ingredients and blend well. Divide the stuffing into 6 portions, place on patties, and top each with a second patty. Press the edges together to seal and remove from waxed paper. Grill over hot coals until done.

# SPAMWAY MULTI-LEVEL CASSEROLE

| | |
|---|---|
| 1 can Spam, diced | 1/2 cup evaporated milk |
| 1 cup cooked rice | 1 can cream of asparagus soup |
| 1/2 cup grated Old English cheese | |

The ingredients should be layered like lasagna. You can double, triple, or quadruple the recipe, but cook in separate pans or the ingredients on bottom will suffocate. Cover with buttered crumbs and cook at 350 degrees for 30-40 minutes.

# STUFFED PIGGIES

| | |
|---|---|
| 4 frankfurters | 8 tbsp. sauerkraut |
| mustard | 1/2 cup apple sauce |
| 1 slice American cheese, | 4 bacon strips |
|    cut into 4 strips | 4 hot dog buns |

If you like German cuisine, you'll love sauerkraut and applesauce hot dogs. Substitute large Polish sausages for an even more authentic Bavarian experience. My neighbor, Hilda von Siddau, from Argentina, is crazy about these. She joined the church in 1950 and immigrated to Utah but fell away in mid-1978. I'm sure she'll see the light again someday, especially now that our Heavenly Father has re-opened Eastern Europe to the gospel.

Slit the hot dogs lengthwise to make a pocket and brush with mustard. Mix the apple sauce and sauerkraut. Place strip of cheese and 2 tablespoons of apple sauce and sauerkraut mixture along each slit. Spiral wrap bacon around each dog and fasten with toothpicks. Grill over hot coals until bacon is crisp and serve on hot dog buns.


# SWEET AND SOUR HOT DOGS

| | |
|---|---|
| 1 pkg. hot dogs | 1/2 cup ketchup |
| 1/2 cup apple or currant jelly | |

Cut the hot dogs into pieces. Melt jelly and ketchup together in a sauce pan, add the hot dogs, and simmer for 20 minutes until the sauce thickens. You may want to add curry and serve over rice with a side-dish of your favorite chutney.

*Fun's a popp'n.*

# JONAH'S SEAFOOD CASSEROLE

| | |
|---|---|
| **1 box frozen fish sticks** | **1 can cream of chicken soup** |
| **1 box frozen chopped broccoli** | **1 can tuna** |
| **1 can sliced water chestnuts** | **1 cup bread crumbs** |
| **1 can cream of mushroom soup** | **1 4 oz. can parmesan cheese** |

At our home we have seafood casserole every Friday. It's quick and easy, and I can whip it together while dressing for an evening with LaMar at our favorite all-you-can-eat buffet and community theater.

Combine soups, broccoli, water chestnuts, and tuna. Pour into 9x13 pan. Place fish sticks upright into the mixture. This gives the effect of fish jumping out of water! Sprinkle bread crumbs and parmesan over the top. Bake at 350 degrees 20-25 minutes. See how easy fish can be!

# TUNA À LA KING OF KINGS

*Mark 6:41*

| | |
|---|---|
| **1 can peas** | **1 cup milk** |
| **1/4 cup margarine** | **1/2 cup cream** |
| **1/4 cup flour** | **4 oz. can sliced mushrooms, drained** |
| **1/2 tsp. salt** | **1 6 oz. can, albacore tuna, drained** |
| **1/4 tsp. dry mustard** | **2 tsp. pimento, chopped** |
| **1/8 tsp. pepper** | |

A Near Eastern tradition at the Christensen home, Tuna à la King of Kings is delicious and inspirational. Despite the New Testament flavor, follow the letter, not the spirit, of the recipe.

Drain the can of peas, reserving 1/2 cup of liquid. Melt margarine on top of a double boiler over low heat. Blend in flour, salt, mustard, and pepper until mixture bubbles. Remove from heat. Gradually add the pea liquid, milk, and cream. Return to heat and bring to a boil, stirring constantly. Cook 1-2 minutes longer and blend in the peas, mushrooms, tuna, and pimento. Cook over low heat until heated thoroughly. Serve over toast, biscuits, noodles, rice, or whatever inspires you. Makes about 3 cups.

*Lip-smacking treats*

# ALOHA PIZZA CASSEROLE

| | |
|---|---|
| 1 32 oz. bottle spaghetti sauce | 1 can pineapple chunks |
| 1 lb. crushed Ritz crackers | 2 cups grated Velveeta cheese |
| 1 can Spam (cut into 1/2-inch cubes) | |

Some people don't know about our great Mormon leader, Walter Murray Gibson, who was prime minister of Hawaii. Unfortunately Brother Gibson got a bit carried away with "temple mistresses" and infallibility doctrines and was sent on a one-way outrigger to the mainland at gunpoint. Yet the plantations our church still operates memorialize his vision of how to exploit the islands' raw, unrealized, natural human potential.

In his honor, add Ritz crackers to three-fourths of the spaghetti sauce and mix until pasty. Begin layering sauce, two-thirds of the Spam, two-thirds of the pineapple, and two-thirds of the cheese until pizza sauce is used. Add final spaghetti sauce and garnish with remaining Spam, pineapple, and cheese. On a warm summer evening, you may think you're at the Polynesian Cultural Center, where LaMar and I spent our honeymoon.

# Let Freedom Ring!

❤

We Mormons have suffered so much over the years to preserve our freedom. Thousands of our forefathers and foremothers walked from Nauvoo, Illinois, to Salt Lake City, starting in 1846. They did this because our religion is based on free agency—and that, brothers and sisters, is the essence of the gospel.

As we all know, in the pre-existence Satan presented a plan that he would come to earth and force us to do good. He would get everyone back to heaven safe and sound. Our older brother Jesus presented his plan—that he would teach us about good and evil and let us choose for ourselves. Free agency was more important than security. While writing the "Let Freedom Ring" section I have been inspired to ponder: Do our politicians know which plan was chosen?

Some people won't know that in Utah we celebrate independence twice in one month—on the 4th of July and on the 24th of July, which is Pioneer Day. No wonder we Mormons have been blessed with so many wonderful barbecue recipes. I'm proud as punch to share them.

*Spamtastic!*

# PEARLS BEFORE SWINE

**1 can Spam (cut into 1-inch cubes)**     **toothpicks**
**2 dozen pearl onions**

Shish-kebab at its best, although you may want to substitute lamb to be kosher. Alternate the onions and Spam cubes on toothpicks. Barbecue on medium hot coals until Spam sizzles and onions are tender. You may also alternate thinly sliced liver and bacon (piggy-back) soaked in barbecue sauce, also sweet peppers and tomatoes.


# LEGISLATURE WEENIES

**eggs**                              **margarine, mustard, ketchup,**
**1 lb. breakfast sausages**              **relish, etc.**
**8-10 English muffins**

We must always keep in mind who the true latter-day weenies are: Democrats parading as true Saints in our state legislature. Grill the miniature weenies over medium hot coals 12-15 minutes while frying the hashbrowns and cooking the eggs (splashed) in a skillet. Lightly toast the English muffins and add condiments, hashbrowns, and a basted egg on top. It may be a little hard on the arteries, but they say there are benefits.

*Train them young . . .*

# KOLOB KEBABS

**1 lb. liver, thinly sliced**          **8 small white onions**
**4 slices bacon**          **favorite barbecue sauce**
**1 cubed sweet pepper**

Kolob is where Heavenly Father lives, and on his many visits to the Middle East, he must have had shish kebab (minus the pork).

Cut the liver into 1-inch strips. Place bacon on a flat surface. Top each piece with 1 or 2 pieces of liver, threaded accordion-style on skewers along with peppers and onions, alternating until the skewer is filled. Brush with barbecue sauce and grill on hot coals until bacon is crisp. Do not overcook.

# ADAM'S BARBECUED SHORT RIBS

**4 lbs. beef short ribs**          **1/4 cup vinegar**
**2 tsp. salt**          **2 tbsp. prepared mustard**
**1/4 tsp. black pepper**          **1/2 cup chopped onion**
**1 can (8 oz.) tomato sauce**          **1 clove garlic (or more), minced**
**1/4 cup ketchup**          **1 tbsp. chili powder**
**1/3 cup packed brown sugar**

My Baptist neighbor Betty says her recipe is as old as Methuselah, and I don't doubt her since she comes from Missouri, which we know is where the Garden of Eden was. But since Cain, who still wanders the earth as Bigfoot, was Adam's son, I doubt that Adam was so short. Still I try to humor my gentile friends since they don't know any better.

Place the short ribs in a covered skillet, and grill slowly over low heat for one and one-half hours, turning occasionally. Season with salt and pepper. In a small sauce pan, combine all other ingredients and bring to a boil over medium heat, stirring frequently. Reduce heat, simmer five minutes, and dip ribs in sauce, coating all sides. Barbecue on grill over low heat 20-30 minutes or until done, turning and brushing with sauce occasionally.

*With a glory in her bosom*
*that transfigures you and me . . .*

# THE PERFECT JUICY BEEFBURGER

## *Can't touch this!*

Remember the cardinal rule for ground beef: Don't overhandle your meat. Some people moosh and mash it until all the juice oozes out and it's just a shadow of what it once was. The more you handle it, the tougher it becomes.

Place on medium hot coals—don't let it get too hot. When juice appears, in 5-6 minutes, turn only once. Cook another 5-6 minutes while getting your buns ready. Add the condiments to the buns, not the burgers.

For rare done, cook 10-12 minutes; for medium done, 14-15 minutes. Avoid cooking longer than 15 minutes. Well-done is an abomination. As I like to remind people: "Your burnt offerings are not acceptable to me, saith the Lord of Hosts and Hostesses."

# SECRET COMBINATION PLATE

## *A platter to relish!*

4 small zucchini, quartered
  lengthwise
1 red bell pepper, cut into spears
1 green bell pepper, cut into spears
1 yellow bell pepper, cut into spears
1 large sweet potato, cross-cut into
  circles 1/4-inch thick
2 medium yellow summer squash,
  quartered lengthwise

1 medium yellow onion, sliced
  1/2-inch thick
1 dozen pearl onions, pierced
1 dozen cherry tomatoes, pierced
1 stick butter
1 clove garlic, crushed
1/4 tsp. black pepper
1/2 tsp. salt

If someone spreads gossip about you, leave this lovely platter of garden goods on their doorstep. It will unlock the door to their heart without awkward handshakes or promises.

Combine the butter, garlic, pepper, and salt over low heat until the butter is melted. Barbecue the vegetables on grill until tender, brushing with butter mixture. Arrange on a large platter and serve as a side dish.

# Mock Cooking and Quick Foods

♥

**I** love masquerades. It's fun to watch people's faces when they're not sure what they're eating. Of course, everyone has to decide for herself the ethics of concealing ingredients, but I like to play "coy hostess" and let people guess.

*Only another fifty bags . . .*

# HUSH-UMS

### *Baby sitter in a baggie!*

**Cherrios**                                    **twist-ties**
**Lucky Charms**                         **plastic bags, sandwich size**
**Fruit Loops**

What a life saver these can be at Sunday School—like sugar cubes at a zoo. Mix the cereals as evenly as possible in a large bowl. Fill the plastic bags with 1/2 cup portions, and twist closed with ties. I recommend carrying 5 or 6 at a time in your pockets or purses for toddlers. It's also nice to have some in food storage as a reserve, but make sure they are easily accessible. If your child is hyperactive, it may be best to omit the Fruit Loops.


# MOCK OYSTER DIP

**1 stick melted butter**                  **dash cayenne pepper**
**1 small onion, chopped**              **dash kitchen bouquet**
**1 can mushroom soup**                **1 pkg. frozen, chopped broccoli,**
**1 can mushrooms, chopped**              **thawed**
**1 8 oz. jar Cheese Whiz**

If your family turns up their noses at fish, this doesn't taste anything like seafood, which is the beauty of it. Sauté the onion in butter. Mix other ingredients and simmer 15 minutes. Add mushrooms last.

*1st Prize*

# QUICK MOCK LASAGNA

**Ritz crackers**                    **ketchup**
**American cheese (sliced singles)**

This will be your children's favorite. I included it at the urging of my son, Shirl, who truly has been an inspiration to me throughout this project. Place about a dozen Ritz crackers on a microwaveable plate. Make sure there are no spaces between the crackers. Layer the Ritz crackers with the cheese slices, then spread ketchup over the cheese with a spoon. Repeat this process so that you have two layers of everything. Microwave for 2-3 minutes. Serve with garlic bread and grape Kool Aid.


# MOCK CHICKEN LEGS

**12 hard bread sticks (about 4 inches in length)**

**4 chicken bullion cubes**

**2 cups finely crushed Ritz crackers**

**2 eggs, well beaten**

**1/2 cup milk**

**chicken spices (salt, pepper, garlic, onion powder, etc.)**

**1 cup water**

**1 cup coarsely crushed corn flakes**

They look like drumsticks, taste like chicken, and are tender as fresh Spam. All in all, they're better than the real thing. It's like buying wrinkle-free polyester instead of cotton. Dissolve chicken bullion cubes in water and simmer. Add water, 1/4 cup at a time, to Ritz crackers, stirring after each addition to smooth. Add water until mixture is a thick paste. Form the mixture into 2-inch balls on the end of each breadstick to form mini drumsticks. Add spices and milk to eggs and beat. Baptize each breadstick in the beaten egg mixture. Now it's time for the laying on of corn flakes. Roll each drumstick in flakes and place on lightly oiled baking sheet. Bake at 300 degrees for about 20 minutes. Serve with generous helpings of instant mashed potatoes.

*LAMAR !?&*$#@!*

# LUMPY DICK

1 cup flour                           2 cups milk
1 egg                               sugar

The older the sister, the better acquainted she will be with this pioneer treat that has been handed down by word-of-mouth. We veterans are grateful to Sister Dick who memorialized her dear husband by naming these sweet dumplings after him.

Whip the egg slightly with a fork and stir into flour until lumps form. It's okay if some of the flour remains unmoistened by the egg. Pour mixture into hot, scalded milk. Cook and let thicken, stirring enough to keep it from sticking. Serve in bowls with milk and sugar. "Beneath a bough, a glass of milk, sweet lumpy dick, and thou."

# MOCK PECAN PIE

1 cup white sugar            1 1/2 cups white corn syrup
1 cup brown sugar            4 eggs, beaten
1 cup butter, melted         2 tsp. vanilla
2 cups milk                     1 cup coconut
1 1/2 cups oatmeal

You may find pecans difficult to come by out of season, but oatmeal is always available. Besides, oat kwiz-een is one of nature's little whisk brooms and we could all use a little cleaning from time to time. Mix all of the ingredients together, pour into four unbaked pie shells, bake at 375 degrees for 40 minutes, and serve with your favorite non-dairy whipped topping.

# MOCK PATÉ

1 can Spam, cubed

1 can Vienna sausages

1/2 cup mayonnaise

1/2 cup chopped olives

1/2 cup chopped celery

1/2 cup pickle relish

1/2 cup chopped onion

This is a formal dining appetizer, best accompanied by crackers and grape juice at room temperature. Thoroughly pulverize the Spam and Vienna sausages in a food processor. Then add the remaining ingredients and process until thoroughly mixed but not pulverized. For an especially elegant evening, serve with hard-boiled eggs (cooled and crumbled) and capers (or baby peas in a pinch).

# Zucchini

♥

**W**hen life hands you a lemon, make lemonade. When someone hands you a zucchini, your options are unlimited!"

Heavenly Father must love zucchini, there's so much of it, especially in Utah where it helped make the desert "blossom like a rose." But I protest the recent, unseemly practice of dumping surplus zucchini on neighbors' porches under the guise of generosity. How much more thoughtful to leave zucchini pie or zucchini jam. If you allow it, this subtle vegetable can become the truffle in your repertoire of garden greens.

*Hm-m-m!*

# HIDE THE ZUCCHINI BREAD

*When you just don't know where to put it!*

| | |
|---|---|
| 3 eggs | 2 cups sugar |
| 1 cup oil | 2 cups coarsely grated zucchini |
| 1 tsp. soda | 3 tsp. vanilla |
| 3 cups flour | 1 tsp. salt |
| 1/4 tsp. baking powder | 2 tsp. cinnamon |
| 1 cup walnuts, chopped | |

People who would never touch a raw zucchini devour it when it's camouflaged in bread. What a delicious, melt-in-your-mouth delicacy! Beat eggs until foamy. Add sugar, oil, vanilla and zucchini. Mix well. Pour into 3 small greased bread pans. Bake at 350 degrees about 50 minutes or until toothpick comes out clean.

# ZUCCHINI O'GRATIN

| | |
|---|---|
| 2 tbsp. olive or corn oil | 1/4 cup parmesan cheese |
| 3 or 4 tender zucchini, peeled, washed, and cut into thin rounds | 1 sprig fresh parsley, chopped |
| | 1/2 cup bread crumbs |
| 1/2 lb. mozzarella cheese, cubed | 2 tbsp. butter |

My dear friends in Idaho think that O'Gratin implies potatoes, but try my grated cheese and zucchini and judge for yourself. Potatoes are cheap, but people pay you to take their zucchini. Before you begin, remember to preheat your oven to 350 degrees. Pour the oil into an 8-inch baking dish and assemble the zucchini, cheeses, and parsley in layers. Cover with crumbs, dot with butter, and bake uncovered until golden brown (about 45-50 minutes).

*Some zucchini just call your name.*

# LEMON ZUCCHINI COOKIES

2 cups flour
1 tsp. baking powder
1/2 tsp. salt
3/4 cup butter
3/4 cup sugar

1 egg, beaten
1 tsp. lemon peel (more if desired)
1 cup shredded, unpeeled zucchini
1 cup chopped nuts

Recently I was shocked to discover there are places where people have never heard of cookies. When LaMar and I were searching our ancestors in Denmark we couldn't even find ingredients like chocolate chips or peanut butter. We felt it our duty to call Sister Fields back home and recommend a cookie air-drop. I think they would especially benefit from my Lemon Zucchini Cookies.

To transform your garden into cookies, stir the flour, baking powder, and salt together and set aside. In a large bowl, cream together the butter and sugar until light. Add the egg and lemon peel and beat until fluffy. At low speed or with a spatula, stir in the flour mixture until the dough is smooth, then stir in the zucchini and chopped nuts. Drop by spoonfuls on a greased cookie sheet and bake at 375 degrees for 15-20 minutes until lightly brown.

# ZUCCHINI JAM

4 cups peeled, ground zucchini, well
   drained
1/2 cup lemon juice
2 pkgs. raspberry Jell-O

8 cups sugar
1 20 oz. can unsweetened pineapple
   juice
1 pkg. pectin

I feel good about using native ingredients. Also, zucchini breaks the monotony of strawberry jam and grape jelly. I can't imagine how people survived on such limited, uninspired choices. Heat the zucchini, lemon juice, and Jell-O together, then let cool. Add the unsweetened pineapple juice and pectin, bring to a boil, add sugar, and boil 5 minutes. Makes 10 pints.

*LaMar's prize zucchini*

# ZUCCHINI RELISH

6 fresh zucchini, cubed

3 green sweet peppers, cut

3 red sweet peppers, cut

5 large onions, cut

5 cups sugar

2 tbsp. mustard seed

4 tsp. tumeric

6 cups dark cider vinegar

1 tbsp. celery seed

7 tbsp. flour

Take this to the state fair and you'll be crowned Zucchini Queen. Put the zucchini and onions in a pan, cover with water, salt, and ice cubes. Let stand until ice melts. Drain, add sweet peppers, and put in jars. Next combine the sugar, mustard seeds, tumeric, cider, celery seed, and flour. Bring to a boil and cook 1 minute, then pour syrup into jars and seal.

# CHOCOLATE ZUCCHINI CAKE

3 eggs

1 cup oil

2 cups sugar

2 cups grated, raw zucchini

3 tsp. vanilla

3 cups flour

1 tsp. salt

1 tsp. soda

1/2 cup cocoa

1/2 tsp. baking powder

1/2 cup nuts

Zucchini adds complexity and moistness without overwhelming or diluting the rich chocolate. Begin by beating the eggs, then add oil, sugar, vanilla, and grated zucchini. Blend. Add all dry ingredients and blend. Put in 2 greased loaf pans lined on bottom with wax paper. Bake at 325 degrees for 1 hour. Serve with milk.

*Zucchini's great in pancakes.*
*Batter's up!*

# ZUCCHINI PIE

2 cups peeled, chopped zucchini

1 cup sugar

1 stick margarine

1/4 cup lemon juice

1/2 tsp. salt

1 tsp. cinnamon

1 unbaked 9-inch pie crust

Believe it or not, this tastes exactly like apple pie, with the appearance of zucchini but lacking the flavor thereof. I imagine when the elders of Zion rescue the Constitution, they will come back praising Old Glory, Mom, and Zucchini Pie. When you want to spoil your loved ones and store up treasures in heaven, try this. Assemble the ingredients and mix with melted margarine, then cook on low heat for 5 minutes, stirring constantly. Pour into the pie crust to bake at 350 degrees for 30-40 minutes. Then top with—what else?—vanilla ice milk.

# ZUCCHINI RICE CASSEROLE

1/2 cup rice

1 chopped onion

3-4 zucchini, cut in 1/4-in. slices

1/2 diced green peppers

1 8 oz. can tomato sauce

1 cup grated cheddar cheese

1/4 cup parmesan cheese

We're not on best terms with Japan right now, but if we produced quality products like my Zucchini Rice Casserole the terrible trade deficit would vanish.

Cook the rice and onion together for 20 minutes. Cook zucchinis and green pepper in boiling water for 5 minutes. Drain well. Mix everything with tomato sauce, pour into a baking dish, and top with cheddar and parmesan cheeses. Bake at 325 degrees for 30 minutes. *Itadakimasu!*

*Don't panic . . .*

*Put your shoulder to the wheel.*

*Who'd guess these were once zucchini?*

# Beverages
### (void of spirit)

♥

**M**y first experience with fine dining was at Chez Roger's in Rexburg, Idaho. I ordered Coq au Vin, thinking it was something with chocolate, not dreaming there would be alcohol in it. When the *sommelier* arrived, I didn't dare order anything but water. I've since learned that even worldly diners stock cranberry juice. But as I sat in Chez Roger's and watched the gentiles sip their mint juleps and cappucinos, I thought, Why should Mormons be treated like second-class citizens? We should create the drinks the gentiles clamor for. So I put my mind to work and came up with a few.

*I will follow him . . .*

# MAUVE WEDDING PUNCH

*Guaranteed to match your bridesmaids' dresses!*

**2 large cans pineapple juice**
**2 small cans frozen lemonade**
**1 half gal. pineapple sherbet**

**1 1/2 large bottles ginger ale**
**1 pkg. red Kool Aid**

Let's face it, at wedding receptions people expect something special in the punch bowl. The frothy sherbet and ginger ale add just the right touch. For Halloween, I add a piece of dry ice and the children are spell-bound.

# SUPPRESSO

**1 cup boiling water**

**4 tbsp. instant Postum**

What people seem to like about "hot drinks" such as espresso and café au lait is the soothing effect on the tummy. I find Postum makes me calm and content without caffeine jitters. Converts to the Lord's one true church find that Postum helps them resist the coffee temptation, which is why I call this Suppresso.

*Gold and Green Ball?*
*I was the queen!*

# GOLD AND GREEN BALLS

1 qt. lime sherbet

1 qt. pineapple sherbet

3 16 oz. bottles lemon lime soda

In Utah Valley, the most lavish and eagerly anticipated social event of the year used to be the autumn Gold and Green Ball. I remember the words of one stunning debutante who summed up what this occasion meant for us girls: "We Mormons like to do things in a big way. When we have families, we have big families. When we have weddings, we have big weddings. When we have balls, we have big balls!" My favorite drink at the soda fountain where we'd stop after the dance was pineapple fizz.

Using a melon baller, roll small scoops of sherbet and fill glasses. Pour lemon lime soda over sherbet. Serve with spoons and straws.

# FIRESIDE WHIZZ

1 pkg. lemon-lime Kool Aid

1/2 cup sugar or more to taste

1 quart milk

1 pint vanilla ice cream

1 16 oz. bottle lemon-lime
carbonated beverage, chilled

Real ice cream is imperative. Thou shalt not substitute ice milk or low-fat yogurt.

Get a family size bowl to combine the Kool Aid, sugar, and milk. Stir to dissolve Kool Aid and sugar and add ice cream by spoonfuls. Carefully pour in the lemon-lime carbonated beverage, and serve immediately. Makes 12-16 servings.

*So young, so fresh.*

# ANTELOPE ISLAND ICED TEA

1 diet Pepsi                          1 diet Mountain Dew
1 diet Dr. Pepper                     1 diet Coca-Cola

I feel so industrious when I sip this luxurious drink. Mix and serve over ice in tall glasses with a twist of lemon. It's almost as potent as the real thing.

# IRISH POSTUM

1 cup Postum, sweetened               1 mint sprig garnish
1 dollop non-dairy whipped topping    1 potato wedge

After a meal, it's always nice to have a warm drink with dessert. This can also be served cold as an appetizer.

# PRUNE JULIUS

1 qt. orange juice    milk, to taste
1 qt. prune juice     crushed ice

This enchanting nightcap can be served either hot or cold. Serves 2. You can substitute Tang for orange juice.

# SURELY TEMPLE

1 can ginger ale     1 maraschino cherry
1 tbsp. maraschino cherry juice  ice

If you saw *Babette's Feast*, you know that dinner can be a spiritual experience, as with our cherry and ginger ale punch.

To prepare, put on your favorite Mormon Tabernacle Choir recording, mix the ginger ale, cherry juice, and cherries, add ice and serve.

# HOT VEGGIE PUNCH

2 cans condensed beef bouillon
2 cans water
5 cups tomato juice
6 ribs celery with leaves

2 small white onions
1 small bay leaf
1 carrot, cut into slices
1 sprig, parsley

As the scripture says, it's good hot or cold, but if it's lukewarm spit it out. Don't be shy with the onions. A little Tabasco goes a long way as well. This is definitely not for gringos.

Simmer together 30-40 minutes. Season to taste. Serve hot with a garnish of lemon slice on a cup.


# JOSEPH AND EMMA'S AFTERNOON DELIGHT

1 can sliced peaches with juice
1 6 oz. can frozen lemonade
   concentrate

1 can 7-Up
ice cubes, to taste

It used to be that Mormons were allowed alcohol for stamina. Brandy was on hand for house raisings, and gin was often a missionary's only traveling companion. This, I'm reliably told, is why there was never a shortage of volunteers. Lounging on the front porch, I find that 7-Up works just fine.

Put all ingredients in a blender. Blend until smooth.

*Sipping my way to a clean house.*

# LEGRAND RICKY

1 cup milk

1 scoop ice cream

2 scoops lime sherbet

3 tbsp. frozen grape juice
concentrate

One of the sweetest men I ever met was Elder LeGrand Richards. As a speaker he was famous, especially for his uplifting, inspirational stories. LaMar and I used to see him at Snelgrove's Ice Cream parlor in Salt Lake City, invariably accompanied by young Thomas Monson. He especially loved grape milk shakes, which is why I named this drink after him.

Mix milk, ice cream, and grape juice in a blender. Pour into a tall glass. Add scoops of sherbet and serve with a spoon and straw.

# FAMILY JULEP

1 can lemon-lime soda

2 tbsp. apple juice

1 tbsp. peach nectar

mint sprigs

We sit on the front porch on our wedding anniversary and sip sweet juleps. It's an excuse to relax and think about how good life has been to LaMar and me.

Prepare by mulling a mint sprig in the bottom of a tall glass. Add liquids and stir slightly. Add ice and top with a mint sprig.

*It's smo-o-o-o-th!*

# *Just Desserts*

❤

**L**aMar and I feel so lucky to live in the dessert capital of the world. Outside of Switzerland, Utah is said to have more chocolate factories, ice cream manufacturers, confectioners, and pastry shops per block than anywhere else. BYU students, bless their hearts, consume more candy per capita than any other student body. This is because they're busy doing good works, as signified by our state emblem the beehive. Others may finish their meals with coffee or brandy, but in Utah we are free to indulge in rich, yummy sweets to our hearts' content, as long as we remain active in our Heavenly Father's work.

*Serve in a decorator cup.*

# ENDOW MINTS

**tooth paste**                    **pastry bag, decorator tips**

These inspiring treats are not only refreshing but help prevent tooth decay. In Heavenly Father's church, "endowment" means cleanliness and empowerment, which makes it an appropriate name for these extra-special mints. Fill a pastry bag with your favorite toothpaste. Using assorted decorator tips, pipe onto wax paper in the shape of your favorite temple. Let dry uncovered for three days. Remove from wax paper and place in candy dishes.

# TOMATO SOUP CAKE

**1/4 cup shortening**              **1 tsp cinnamon**
**1 cup sugar**                     **1 tsp nutmeg**
**1 can tomato soup**              **1/2 tsp cloves**
**1 tsp baking soda**              **10 maraschino cherries, cut up**
**2 cups flour**                    **nuts, optional**
**1 1/2 tsp baking powder**

I say "toe-may-toe," LaMar says "toe-mah-toe"; let's make Tomato Soup Cake. When you have a can of Campbell's in the cupboard, it's like tithing in the bank. We've already encountered this versatile product in casseroles, meat entrees, breads, and beverages: what a delight to find it in a cake!

Heat soup (after opening the can), add baking soda, and set aside to cool. Cream shortening and sugar. Sift dry ingredients together with flour. Add soup mixture and dry ingredients and about 1/2 cup water or as much as needed. Pour into a greased 9x9x2 pan and bake at 350 degrees for 45 minutes. I like to serve Tomato Soup Cake warm, sans icing. One healthy mouthful and you'll be saying "toe-m-ahhh!-toe," too.

*Precious in His sight.*

# NEPHITE AND LAMANITE COOKIES

| | |
|---|---|
| 1 cup flour | 1 cup sugar |
| 2 heaping tsp. cocoa | 2 eggs |
| 1 stick melted butter | 1 tsp. vanilla |
| 1 cup chopped nuts | |

The Book of Mormon says originally there were two Indian tribes, the Nephites, who were "white and delightsome," and the Lamanites, who were "cursed with a dark skin." The Lamanites fared better, probably because of their natural sun screen. These tribes can be represented in ginger-bread fashion, which is an especially appropriate activity for children.

First, mix sugar and melted butter in a sauce pan. Add eggs and flour. Separate into two equal portions. In one pan, add cocoa, in the other, vanilla. Mix well. The mixtures will be thick. Fashion into human shapes using nuts where appropriate. Bake at 300 degrees for 30 minutes.

While baking, put 1 tbsp. butter each into two separate saucepans, add 2 tbsp. cocoa to one and 2 tbsp. vanilla to the other. Mix and cook separately. Remove from heat, add 1 tbsp. hot water to each and stir. Add 1/2 cup powdered sugar and 1 tsp. vanilla each. Decorate the hot cookies, fashioning hair and clothing. With food coloring, apply war paint.

# CHOCOLATE MAYONNAISE CAKE

| | |
|---|---|
| 2 cups cake flour | 1/4 tsp. salt |
| 1 cup sugar | 1 cup mayonnaise |
| 2 tsp. baking soda | 1 cup cold water |
| 1/2 cup cocoa | 1 tsp. vanilla |

Out of milk, eggs, and shortening the day before payday? Reach for the mayonnaise! As they say, poverty is the mother-in-law of invention. Sift together flour, sugar, baking soda, cocoa, and salt. Fold in mayonnaise, water, and vanilla. Pour into 2 greased 8-inch layer pans and bake at 350 degrees for 30 minutes.

Serve with a knowing smile. With this rich dessert, your family will never guess you spent the shopping money on lottery tickets in Malad.

*Seagulls with cricket filling*

# SEA GULLS

| | |
|---|---|
| 2 cups flour | 1 tsp. vanilla |
| 1 cup shortening | 2 tbsp. flour |
| 1 cup sugar | 2/3 cup sugar |
| 3 tsp. baking powder | 1 cup raisins |
| 1/2 tsp. salt | |

Historians say that sea gulls devoured crickets to save the settlers' crops in Baja California, not Salt Lake City. Wherever it happened, it was a miracle. Combine the flour, shortening, sugar, baking powder, salt, and vanilla. Roll thin and cut into sea gull shapes.

For cricket filling, combine 2 tbsp. flour, 2/3 cup sugar, raisins, and 1 cup boiling water. Place between cookies and bake at 350 degrees for 10 to 12 minutes. This treat is appropriate for Pioneer Day or Cinco de Mayo.

# SATAN FOOD CAKE

| | |
|---|---|
| 3 oz. (3 squares) chocolate | 1 cup milk |
| 2 cups sifted cake flour | 1/2 tsp. red food coloring |
| 1 tsp. baking soda | 12 oz. semi-sweet chocolate chips |
| 1/2 tsp. salt | 1 cup thick sour cream |
| 1/2 cup butter | 1 tsp. vanilla |
| 1 1/2 tsp. vanilla | 1/4 tsp. almond extract |
| 1 1/2 cups light brown sugar | 1/8 tsp. salt |
| 2 eggs, well beaten | |

LaMar is convinced the devil made me include this one. It's a little decadent but tastes so good it can't be all bad.

Grease and flour two 8-inch round cake pans. Melt chocolate squares and set aside. Sift together dry ingredients and set aside. Cream together butter, vanilla, and sugar. Add eggs in thirds. Stir in cooled chocolate. Alternately add dry ingredients in fourths and milk in thirds. After each addition, beat until smooth; blend in food coloring with last strokes. Turn batter into pans, bake at 350 degrees 30-35 minutes. Melt chocolate chips and cool, blending into sour cream. Add almond extract, vanilla, and salt.

*Oops!*

# BURNING BOSOMS

3 large grapefruits  
6 maraschino cherries  
brown sugar  

rum (borrowed from a gentile  
neighbor; it burns out)

This is one of those recipes suited to *Babette's Feast.* It makes you tingle all over and not because of the rum.

Cut the grapefruits in half and place in a serving dish. Sprinkle with brown sugar and top each with a cherry. Add 1-2 tablespoons of rum to each grapefruit. Ignite and serve. Note: if you feel the sweetness of your spirit will be damaged by using alcohol, omit the rum and broil the grapefruits until sizzling. Serves six.


# PEACH MAGNA

1/2 cup raspberry jam  
1 can sliced peaches  
1 box Vanilla Wafers  

1 small container non-dairy whipped  
topping

Poor Magna, Utah, built on a landfill. Few cities are so maligned. But you can't grow a better orchard anywhere in the state without artificial fertilizer.

Drain the Magna peaches, reserving the juice. Arrange peaches and vanilla wafers on a small plate or dessert bowl. Mix raspberry jam and peach juice. Spoon over peaches and vanilla wafers. Place a dollop of whipped topping on each.

*Scriptures are my bag.*

# SCRIPTURE CAKE

## *A hidden treasure*

2 cups Jeremiah 6:20

1 cup Judges 5:25, last clause

6 Jeremiah 17:11

2 tbsp. 1 Samuel 14:25

1/2 cup Judges 4:19, last clause

1 pinch Leviticus 2:13

4 1/2 cups 1 Kings 9:22, first clause

4 tsp. Amos 4:15

1 cup 1 Samuel 30:12, second clause

1 cup 2 Nahum 3:12

1 cup Numbers 17:8

1 cup 2 Chronicles 9:9

A great way to brush up on Bible study, cream Jeremiah 6:20 and Judges 5:25. Add beaten Jeremiah 17:11, 1 Samuel 14:25, and Judges 4:19. Sift together dry ingredients and add to mixture. Beat thoroughly and add 1 Samuel 30:12, Nahum, Numbers, and 2 Chronicles. Bake at 350 degrees for 45 minutes. Be careful not to spill cake mix on your Bible, or you could end up with a sealed portion.

# SWEET POTATO BALLS

3 cups cooked yams

1/4 cup margarine

3/4 cup brown sugar

2 tbsp. milk

1/4 tsp. salt

1/2 tsp. grated lemon rind

8 marshmallows

1/2 cup crushed corn flakes

Of all desserts, this is surely my grandest. LaMar suspects this recipe was slipped to me through the veil. If you have Irish blood you'll find these balls particularly appealing.

Mash the yams. Add margarine, sugar, milk, salt, and lemon rind. Roll into balls around marshmallows and then roll these in corn flakes. Place in a greased baking dish and cover with foil. Bake in slow oven for 20 minutes until marshmallows ooze out.

*Hate is not a family value.*

# SUGAR CUBE TEMPLE

## *A theme treat!*

26,000 sugar cubes
1 gallon corn syrup
4 quarts marshmallow creme
1 dozen egg whites
1 cup granulated sugar

1 marzipan Moroni from Mormon
    handicraft store
1 Salt Lake Temple plan obtained
    from church archives
scale: 1 sugar cube = 1 cubic foot

LaMar and I construct sugar cube temples for family reunions, weddings, and funerals. It's so glorious, people just stand and stare. If it's your first time at a temple, allow six hours.

Mix the corn syrup and marshmallow creme and set aside to use for mortar later. On grid paper, follow the construction plan, stopping sugar cube construction at the Solemn Assembly Room. Beat egg whites and add 1 cup granulated sugar until stiff peaks form. Now form egg whites into 6 large meringue spires on a greased cookie sheet. Broil until light brown. Place 3 spires each on east and west ends of temple base. Place marzipan Moroni on east, center spire. Spotlight and serve.

# POSTUM FROSTING

1 tsp. instant Postum

2 tsp. vanilla

Postum may not be mocha, but it's a lot safer, and you can, in good conscience, serve this to your bishop. Dissolve Postum in vanilla and add to your favorite butter frosting recipe.

*Finally . . . a consensus.*

# UGLY DUCKLING CAKE

| | |
|---|---|
| 1 pkg. yellow cake mix | 1/2 cup brown sugar |
| 1 can fruit cocktail | 1/2 cup margarine |
| 2 1/2 cups flaked coconut | 1/2 cup sugar |
| 2 eggs | 1/2 cup evaporated milk |

Why an ugly duckling? Make it and see. Mix the fruit and syrup, 1 cup coconut, eggs, and cake mix, and pour into a greased 9x13 pan. Sprinkle brown sugar on top and bake at 325 degrees for 45 minutes. Boil margarine, sugar, and milk for 2 minutes. Stir in remaining coconut and spoon over hot cake. Serve warm and conceal with ice milk.

# DUMP CAKE

| | |
|---|---|
| 1 1/2 cups flour | 6 tbsp. oil |
| 1 cup sugar | 1 tbsp. vanilla |
| 3 tbsp. cocoa | 1 tbsp. vinegar |
| 1 tsp. soda | 1 cup cold water |
| 1/2 tsp. salt | |

Older brothers and sisters especially love this one because of its suspected laxative powers.

Sift together dry ingredients into a 10-inch pan, making 3 depressions in the mixture. Into one depression, dump oil; in the next, vinegar; in the third, vanilla. Dump cold water over all and mix well with a fork but do not beat. Bake at 350 degrees for 30 minutes. Double recipe for 9x13 pan.

*Roger S. Salazar*                    *Michael G. Wightman*

# *Acknowledgments*

♥

hanks to Marge Young and her daughter Sue Hefferman for their unceasing support and honest criticism; Ann Parson because she never let us forget we promised to write this book; Kim and Gene for helping to finalize our recipe titles; the Erekson sisters for their satirical view of life; and Eric Murdock for his Jell-O recipes.

To Ed and Jackie Salazar for teaching Roger that anything's possible and laughing only when it's funny; for laughing even when their family and friends didn't; and for bearing with and loving Roger when he strayed from their fold. And Roger's sister Cheryn Ross for letting him be, and loving him the most.

To Jack and Elenor Wightman for raising eleven children without losing their enthusiasm and for loving Michael in spite of his bathroom humor. Michael's sisters Pricilla Weaver and Barbara Pomeranze for screaming and laughing so loudly they convinced us this book was born of genius. Michael's brother Chris and wife Julie for their constant support. And finally Susan Olsen, Michael's baby sister, for telling him she would love him no matter what.

Also thanks to Marybeth Raynes for being our sister in the gospel and standing for the truth; Leslie Natrage for covering Roger's derriere at the salon; and Mary and the Morrisons for always including us in their family.

Now the people we paid to help us: Lynn Van Treese for the stunning detail in her set and floral design; Nancy McDermott for risking her career by doing our food preparation; Steven Petersen for keeping his cool through make-up even though Enid was such a flirt; Deborah Hess for helping Enid accessorize; Marilyn Ivory for giving Enid such lovely nails; Connie Disney for lending us her beautiful children (Emmaly and Sol Adams, Augustine Rodriquez, and Beth Swanson); Brent Corcoran for graciously playing our

eldest son, LaRoy, and adding vivaciousness to Enid's personality; Greg Jones and his grandmother for adding authenticity to Enid's voice; Jani Fleet for proofing and contributing a bit of down-home humor. And to the publisher for judiciously omitting some of our more exotic recipes.

Finally to Sister and Brother Christensen for letting us into their world.

# Favorite Recipes
### (notes)